D1537971

FOUNDATIONS OF OUR NATION
ESTABLISHING THE LEGISLATIVE BRANCH

by Tyler Omoth

FOCUS READERS

WWW.FOCUSREADERS.COM

Focus Readers is distributed by North Star Editions:
sales@northstareditions.com | 888-417-0195

Produced for Focus Readers by Red Line Editorial.

Content Consultant: Dr. Gideon Mailer, Associate Professor of History, University of Minnesota Duluth

Photographs ©: Everett Historical/Shutterstock Images, cover, 1; North Wind Picture Archives, 4–5, 7, 9, 13, 15, 16–17, 20–21, 23, 26–27; SuperStock/Glow Images, 10–11; Stock Montage/Archive Photos/Getty Images, 19; Red Line Editorial, 25, 29

ISBN
978-1-63517-247-8 (hardcover)
978-1-63517-312-3 (paperback)
978-1-63517-442-7 (ebook pdf)
978-1-63517-377-2 (hosted ebook)

Library of Congress Control Number: 2017935922

Printed in the United States of America
Mankato, MN
June, 2017

ABOUT THE AUTHOR

Tyler Omoth grew up in the small town of Spring Grove, Minnesota. He has written more than 40 books for young readers. Tyler loves watching sports, particularly baseball, and getting outside for fun in the sunshine. He lives in sunny Brandon, Florida, with his wife, Mary, and their feisty cat, Josie.

TABLE OF CONTENTS

CHAPTER 1

CREATING CONGRESS

In 1783, the American Revolutionary War (1775–1783) officially ended. The United States was now an **independent** country. However, the US government did not work well at first. It had trouble **enforcing** laws. One reason for this problem was that the national government had only one branch.

George Washington celebrates US independence with members of his army.

This branch made laws. But there was no branch to make sure people followed the laws. And there was no branch to solve disagreements about laws.

In 1787, leaders from several states held a meeting in Philadelphia, Pennsylvania. The leaders wanted to improve the national government.

James Madison was one of the people at the meeting. But he wanted to do more than fix the existing government. He wanted to create a whole new government. Other leaders agreed with Madison. They helped him write the US Constitution. This document became official in June 1788.

The meeting to create a new government became known as the Constitutional Convention.

The Constitution split the national government into three branches. The legislative branch would make laws. The executive branch would enforce those laws. And the judicial branch would decide if laws followed the Constitution.

These three branches created a system of checks and balances. This meant no branch would have too much power. For example, the legislative branch would have power over the other two branches. But those branches would also have power over the legislative branch.

The legislative branch is known as Congress. The Constitution calls for two separate **chambers** in Congress. One chamber is the House of Representatives. The other is the Senate. Both chambers are made up of elected officials from each state. These officials **represent** the concerns of the people who elected them.

Members of Congress first met at Federal Hall in New York City.

CHAPTER 2

THE HOUSE OF REPRESENTATIVES

The House of Representatives is the larger of the two chambers. It met for the first time in 1789. At that time, the House had 65 members. Each of the 13 states was given a certain number of representatives. This number was based on the population of each state.

Frederick Muhlenberg of Pennsylvania was the first leader of the House of Representatives.

Each representative in the House serves a two-year **term**. There are no term limits. That means a representative can be reelected over and over.

To serve in the House, a person must be at least 25 years old. Also, the person needs to have been a US citizen for the past seven years. In addition, the person must live in the state he or she represents.

The House of Representatives has many duties. Its main duty is to create new laws. But the House has other powers, too. For instance, the House can impeach government officials. This is when the House accuses an official of a

The House of Representatives decided the 1824 election and chose John Quincy Adams as president.

crime. After a person is impeached, he or she has a trial in the Senate.

In rare cases, the House can decide the presidential election. However, this happens only when one candidate does not win the necessary number of votes.

COUNTING ENSLAVED PEOPLE

When the Constitution was being written, leaders had to decide whether to count enslaved people. This decision would affect each state's official population. And the population affected the number of representatives each state received.

Most enslaved people lived in southern states. Leaders in these states wanted enslaved people to be counted the same as free people. This would increase the population of southern states. As a result, southern states would have more representatives in Congress.

Leaders in northern states disagreed. They did not want to count enslaved people at all. That's because slavery was less common in northern states. By not counting enslaved people,

In the late 1700s, enslaved people were forced to work on farms that produced tobacco, rice, or sugar.

northern states would get more representatives in Congress.

James Madison supported a compromise. "States should feel as little bias as possible, to swell or to reduce the amount of their numbers," he wrote. "States will have opposite interests, which will control and balance each other." In the end, the Constitution said each enslaved person would count as three-fifths of a person. The compromise ended in 1865, when slavery was finally banned.

CHAPTER 3

THE SENATE

The Senate is the other chamber of Congress. When the Senate first met, it had 26 members. Each state has two senators. That means small states have the same number of senators as larger states. This balances the extra representation that larger states have in the House.

Vice President John Adams was the first leader of the Senate.

Each senator serves a six-year term. Similar to the House, the Senate has no term limits. To serve in the Senate, a person must be at least 30 years old. The person needs to have been a US citizen for the past nine years. The person must also live in the state he or she represents.

The Senate creates new laws, just like the House. Another duty is to approve the president's **appointments**. The president can choose people for government jobs. But first, the Senate meets with these people. The senators vote on whether each person should get the job.

The Senate also holds trials for people who have been impeached. If the

The House impeached Supreme Court justice Samuel Chase in 1804, but the Senate found him not guilty.

majority of senators cast a guilty vote, the person is removed from office.

The Senate also approves treaties made with other nations. The executive branch creates the treaty. But it must be approved by two-thirds of the Senate.

CHAPTER 4

FROM IDEA TO LAW

All laws begin as ideas. For example, a person may want to create a new law. Or a person may want to change an existing law. When the person's idea is written out, it becomes a bill.

Anyone can write a bill. Most often, bills are written by members of Congress.

The First US Congress made a law that prevented many nonwhite people from becoming US citizens.

Sometimes they are written by the executive branch. Outside groups can write bills, too.

After a bill is written, it must have a sponsor. The sponsor is a member of Congress. He or she introduces the bill to the House or Senate. The sponsor speaks with other members of the chamber. He or she tries to gain support for the bill.

Next, the bill goes to a committee. Committees are made up of representatives who specialize in one area of law. Examples include education, agriculture, and the military. The committee may make changes to the bill.

The US Army gets its money from tax laws created by Congress.

Or they may decide the bill should not become a law.

If the committee is satisfied with a bill, the full chamber debates it. Representatives explain what they like or dislike about the bill. Then they vote on it.

If a majority votes in favor of the bill, it moves to the other chamber of Congress. That chamber goes through the same process. In some cases, the two chambers may have different versions of the bill. When this happens, the bill goes to another committee. The members make compromises. They come up with a final version of the bill. Then each chamber votes on it.

If the bill passes, it is sent to the president. The president can then sign the bill or **veto** it. If the president signs the bill, it becomes a law. If the bill is vetoed, it goes back to Congress. Then the chambers vote on it again.

If two-thirds of both chambers vote for it, the bill becomes a law. If not, the bill dies.

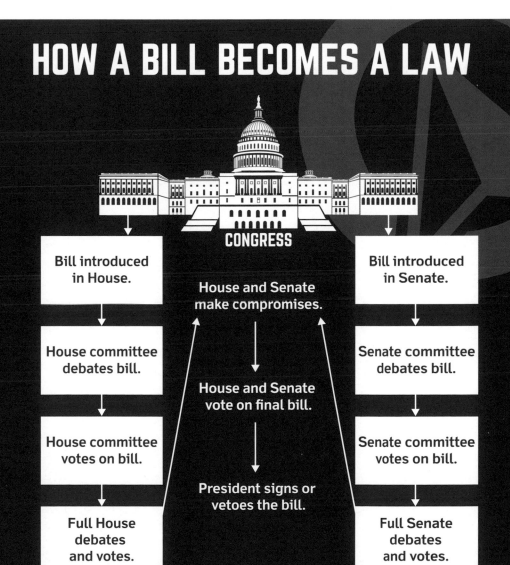

HOW A BILL BECOMES A LAW

CONGRESS

Bill introduced in House.

House committee debates bill.

House committee votes on bill.

Full House debates and votes.

House and Senate make compromises.

House and Senate vote on final bill.

President signs or vetoes the bill.

Bill introduced in Senate.

Senate committee debates bill.

Senate committee votes on bill.

Full Senate debates and votes.

CHAPTER 5

CONGRESS GROWS

The First US Congress faced many important issues. The Constitution was new, and some people believed it needed improvements. Congress does not have the power to change the Constitution. However, Congress can write **amendments**.

James Madison led the effort to amend the Constitution.

An amendment must get approval from two-thirds of both chambers. Then three-fourths of the states have to **ratify** the amendment. If that happens, the Constitution is officially changed. In 1789, Congress approved 12 amendments. By the end of 1791, the states had ratified 10 of them. These 10 amendments became known as the Bill of Rights. They guarantee personal freedoms and limit the power of the government.

As the United States grew, Congress grew with it. Today the House is made up of 435 members. Meanwhile, the Senate has 100 members.

In a three-branch government, the legislative branch is essential. It makes sure people's voices are heard. Representatives then create laws that become the rules of American society.

NUMBER OF REPRESENTATIVES IN EACH STATE (2013–2022)

WA 10
OR 5
MT 1
ND 1
MN 8
VT 1
NH 2
ME 2
ID 2
SD 1
WI 8
NY 27
MA 9
WY 1
IA 4
MI 14
RI 1
NV 4
NE 3
IL 18
IN 9
OH 16
PA 18
CT 5
NJ 12
UT 4
CO 7
KY 6
WV 3
VA 11
DE 1
CA 53
KS 4
MO 8
MD 8
AZ 9
NM 3
OK 5
AR 4
TN 9
NC 13
SC 7
MS 4
AL 7
GA 14
TX 36
LA 6
FL 27
AK 1
HI 2

FOCUS ON
THE LEGISLATIVE BRANCH

Write your answers on a separate piece of paper.

1. Write a paragraph that explains the main ideas of Chapter 4.

2. Do you think it's fair that all states get two senators? Why or why not?

3. How long is a senator's term?

    A. two years
    B. four years
    C. six years

4. When might a bill be sent to a committee?

    A. after the president vetoes the bill
    B. when the House and Senate pass different versions of the bill
    C. before the bill has a sponsor in Congress

Answer key on page 32.

GLOSSARY

amendments
Official changes to a document.

appointments
Selections a president makes to fill government jobs.

chambers
Groups of people who gather to create laws.

enforcing
Making sure people follow a rule.

independent
Having the ability to make decisions without being controlled by another government.

majority
More than half.

ratify
To give official approval.

represent
To speak on behalf of a larger group.

term
The amount of time a person can serve after being elected.

veto
To reject a bill and stop it from becoming a law.

TO LEARN MORE

BOOKS

Bow, James. *What Is the Legislative Branch?* New York: Crabtree Publishing Company, 2013.

Nelson, Robin, and Sandy Donovan. *The Congress: A Look at the Legislative Branch.* Minneapolis: Lerner Publications, 2012.

Spalding, Maddie. *How the Legislative Branch Works.* Mankato, MN: The Child's World, 2016.

NOTE TO EDUCATORS

Visit **www.focusreaders.com** to find lesson plans, activities, links, and other resources related to this title.

INDEX

Answer Key: 1. Answers will vary; **2.** Answers will vary; **3.** C; **4.** B